I0198685

The Birth of God

John Chapter One

The Birth of God

John Chapter One

Dr. Jeffrey D. Johnson
Founder/Director
Israel Today Ministries
P.O. Box 150288
Arlington, TX 76015

RESOURCE *Publications* · Eugene, Oregon

Resource Publications
An imprint of Wipf and Stock Publishers
199 West 8th Avenue, Suite 3
Eugene, OR 97401

The Birth of God
John Chapter One
Copyright©2005 by Dr. Jeffrey D. Johnson
ISBN: 978-1-4982-4770-2
Publication Date: October 2005

All scripture quotations are from the King James version of the Bible.

10   9   8   7   6   5   4   3   2   1

About the Author

Jeffrey D. Johnson is the founder and director of Israel Today Ministries. ITM has a three-fold purpose:

- Teach the Church about Israel
- Teach Israel about their Messiah
- Help feed those in need (Romans 15:27; Genesis 12:1-3)

As an 'Itinerant Teacher', Dr. Johnson will travel anywhere to proclaim God's riches, and redeeming grace through Jesus Christ our Lord.

As a 'Humanitarian', Dr. Johnson is touching thousands with food relief, and the love of Jesus.

As an 'Expositor', Dr. Johnson's teaching focuses on the Jewish roots of Christianity, Bible prophecy, and practical theology.

The late John Walvoord, of Dallas Theological Seminary, said Jeffrey is "an able expositor of the Word of God." Paige Patterson, Bible scholar and seminary president, says Jeffrey is "a practitioner of all that he preaches."

To receive Dr. Johnson's "Teaching Letters" and Middle East updates from Israel Today Ministries contact the address below:

Dr. Jeffrey D. Johnson
Israel Today Ministries
P.O. Box 150288
Arlington, TX 76015

or ITM's web site:

www.israeltodayministries.org

Table of Contents

Preface

The ancients said when the Apostle John, the 'Son of Thunder', who became a 'disciple of love,' was in his eighth and ninth decade of life, the Christians would literally carry John, because of his poor health, from church to church. The early Christian community wanted to hear what the last living apostle had to say. The pastors would ask the sage apostle, " Would you give us a word from the Lord." It is reported that John would simply say, "Love God with all your heart, love each other, and by this all men will know that you are Christ's disciples."

John's focus was the love of God. In chapter one of his magnificent gospel account we find the ultimate expression of God's love: God himself, becoming man dying on a cruel Roman cross, paying the price for redemption.

The great apostle takes us beyond the mountains, past the heavens, and exiting the sidereal universe enters into the heavenly chamber of the Throne of God. There he kneels before God, looking into the heart of the eternal mind of the Almighty, and receives the revelation, thus recording, "In the beginning was the Word, and the Word was with God, and the Word was God."

In the next few pages you will enter the mind of God and experience a universal paradigm shift in God's dealings with man, the Incarnation – the birth of God (in the flesh), and the birth of a movement that changed the world forever.

Part One
John Chapter One

The Son of Thunder

"The Fourth Gospel opens with a magnificent series of apparently metaphysical propositions. The time is the beginning of all things, the theme is the creation, and the substantives denote a sequence of large concepts: God, the Word, light, life, darkness."[1]

"The Gospel of John may be compared to an artesian well that never runs dry. From its depths there bubbles forth clear, refreshing water to quench the thirst of men and women who turn to it in their quest for life's true meaning."[2]

"Within John's Gospel we will find a universal impetus that declares that Jesus is the 'Savior of the world.'

> 'for we have heard Him ourselves, and know that this is indeed the Christ, the Saviour of the world.' John 4:42

John speaks of 'freedom, truth, and love.'"[3]

> "Therefore if the Son makes you free, you shall be free indeed." (8:36)

John gives us the purpose for writing his Gospel in chapter 20:30-31.

> *"And many other signs truly did Jesus in the presence of his disciples, which are not written in this book: But these are written, that ye might believe that Jesus is the Christ, the Son of God; and that believing ye might have life through his name."*

"This statement contains three basic affirmations:

1. The author's central message is related to Jesus, whom he presents to his readers as 'the Christ, the Son of God.'

2. There is an appeal for 'believing' in Jesus. This concept carries for John the connotation of trust and commitment as well as of intellectual assent to a statement of fact.

3. The result of such a personal and positive response will be 'life' in His name."[4]

The word "life" (Greek - *Zoe*) is the most significant word in the Gospel of John. It appears 35 times more than in any other Gospel. John's Gospel is also called the "Gospel of Life".

John's style is not so much a narrative of the Life of Christ as much as a series of sermonic themes and theological treatises which centers around the incarnation, seven miracles, seven "I Am's", faith, unbelief, light, darkness, truth and life.

John's passion is nothing less than profound.

Who Was John?

"In the book the author is identified as the 'beloved disciple' (21:20-24) who sat next to Jesus at the (last) supper. John …was the brother of James, another of the twelve disciples of Jesus, and both were sons of Zebedee. Like his father and older brother, James, he was a fisherman on the Sea of Galilee, and together with Peter and James, John was one of the three disciples closest to Jesus."[5]

Some historians state that John's family business made them relatively wealthy and influential which may explain how he was able to enter the house of Caiaphas during one of the trials of Jesus.

Jesus called James and John 'sons of thunder' (Mark 3:17). They rebuked a man for casting out demons because he was not following them (Mark 9:38). Also, they asked permission to punish the Samaritans with fire from heaven for their inhospitality to Jesus. Later they urged Jesus to give the two of them places of honor in the kingdom to come.

Peter, James and John witnessed events that were not shared by the other apostles such as: the raising of Jairus's daughter, the transfiguration (John 1:14) and Jesus' prayer in the Garden of Gethsemane.

According to Luke it was Peter and John who were sent to prepare the Passover meal (Last Supper).

At the crucifixion John appears standing with Mary, the mother of Jesus. From the cross Jesus said to his mother, 'Woman, behold your son!' (referencing John)…and to the disciple, 'Behold your mother!' And from that hour that disciple took her to his own home.' (19:26,27) Mary would have been in her late 40's or early 50's at this point. She will live the rest of her natural life under the care of John the beloved.

3

Dr. Jeffrey D. Johnson

After Mary Magdalene reported that Jesus' tomb was empty, John with Peter ran to the tomb and after seeing, believed. John was the first to accept Jesus' resurrection.

Later, John was in the group that went fishing with Peter in Galilee. When Jesus appeared on the shore, the beloved disciple was the first to recognize him.

> 'After these things Jesus shewed himself again to the disciples at the sea of Tiberias; and on this wise shewed he himself. There were together Simon Peter and Thomas called Didymus, and Nathanael of Cana in Galilee, and the sons of Zebedee, and two other of his disciples. Simon Peter saith unto them, I go a-fishing. They say unto him, we also go with thee. They went forth, and entered into a ship immediately; and that night they caught nothing. But when the morning was now come, Jesus stood on the shore: but the disciples knew not that it was Jesus. Then Jesus saith unto them, Children, have ye any meat? They answered him, No. And he said unto them, Cast the net on the right side of the ship, and ye shall find. They cast therefore, and now they were not able to draw it for the multitude of fishes. Therefore that disciple whom Jesus loved saith unto Peter, It is the Lord. Now when Simon Peter heard that it was the Lord he girt his fisher's coat unto him, (for he was naked,) and did cast himself into the sea. And the other disciples came in a little ship; (for they were not far from land, but as it were two hundred cubits,) dragging the net with fishes. As soon then as they were come to land, they saw a fire of coals there, and fish laid thereon, and bread. Jesus saith unto them, Bring of the fish which ye have now caught. Simon Peter went up, and drew the net to land full of great fishes, an hundred and fifty and three: and for all there were so many, yet was not the net broken. Jesus saith unto

*them, Come and dine. And none of the disciples durst
ask him, Who art thou? knowing that it was the Lord.
Jesus then cometh, and taketh bread, and giveth them,
and fish likewise. This is now the third time that Jesus
shewed himself to his disciples, after that he was risen
from the dead.' John 21:1-14*

Perhaps John recalled Luke 5:1-11 (when Jesus called them to
'full-time' discipleship…apparently, they initially did not follow
Him on a 'full-time' basis (see Bible Knowledge Commentary).

His brother, James, was the first apostle to be martyred.
John continued for some time as a prominent leader in the early
Christian church. Paul lists John as one of the 'pillars' (Galatians
2:9) of the Jerusalem church. His prominence is also recorded in
the book of Acts, where he is said to have accompanied Peter on
important missions.

*'Now when the apostles which were at Jerusalem heard
that Samaria had received the word of God, they sent
unto them Peter and John.' Acts 8:14*

John authored 1,2,3 John and later in his life he was exiled
to the island of Patmos, after a failed attempt by the authorities
to kill him by boiling him in oil in Ephesus. Terribly scarred, on
this remote island John receives the Revelation of Jesus Christ,
thus the title of the last book of the Bible.

- Not only was John <u>impetuous </u>desiring to destroy the
  Samaritans and coveting an honored position in the
  Kingdom.

- He became a man of <u>compassion</u> and <u>concern</u> as he leaned
  upon the breast of our Lord at the Last Supper and asked,
  "Is it I who will betray You?" *(Matthew 26:22)*

- He also became a man of <u>commitment</u> as he lovingly cared for Mary.

- He also became a man of <u>passion</u> and <u>zeal</u> for the Lord as he cried with enthusiasm on that morning after the resurrection beholding the Master on the shore, "It is the Lord!"

- This one, named John, became a "<u>pillar</u>" of the church.

And with the tenacity and strength of a fisherman, and with the love of a seasoned apostle he gave us an example of persevering until the end of our days embracing truth with a passion manifesting a submission before a holy God. He demonstrated the manifest destiny of every believer when we shall appear before the presence of God (*Revelation 1:9-18*).

John enters the presence of God with grace, dignity and true spirituality in his Gospel.

Augustine writes that John was "among the mountains… "(when he wrote, 'In the beginning was the Word, and the Word was with God, and the Word was God…'

What was this mountain like, how high? It surpassed all earthly summits, it surpassed all the spaces of the air, it surpassed the highest stars, it surpassed all the choirs and all the legions of angels.

If indeed it had not surpassed everything created it would not have come to the One through whom everything has been made (*John 1:3*). You cannot realize what he surpassed unless you see where he arrived."[6]

We will embrace with passion, meditation and worship chapter one of John's crowned 'Gospel of Life'.

We Can Change!

If our Lord can take a rough, crass, cursing fisherman and turn him into a vessel of honor and grace, He can surely change you and me.

He will give hope to you who have no hope.

> *"…lay hold upon the hope set before us. Which hope we have as an anchor of the soul, both sure and stedfast… even Jesus." (Hebrews 6:18-20)*

He will give peace to you who have no peace.

Jesus said, *"Peace I leave with you, My peace I give to you; not as the world gives do I give to you. Let not your heart be troubles, neither let it be afraid." (John 14:27)*

He will give rest to the restless and lift your burden.

Jesus also said, *"Come to Me, all you who labor and are heavy laden, and I will give you rest. Take My yoke upon you and learn from Me, for I am gentle and lowly in heart, and you will find rest for your soul. For My yoke is easy and My burden is light." Matthew 11:28-30*

He will give life to those who believe.

> *"All things were made by Him; and without Him was not any thing made that was made." John 1:3*

> *"The Father loveth the Son, and hath given all things into His hand. He that believeth on the Son hath*

everlasting life: and he that believeth not the Son shall not see life; but the wrath of God abideth on him." John 3:35,36

Choose this day what you will do...Will you believe?

Endnotes

[1] A.E. Harvey, *"Jesus on Trial, A Study in the Fourth Gospel"*, John Knox Press, Atlanta, 1977, p.18.

[2] D. George Vanderlip, *"Christianity According to John"*, (Westminster Press, Philadelphia, 1975), p.9.

[3] Ibid., p.12

[4] Ibid., p.17

[5] James B. Bell, *"The Roots of Jesus, A Genealogical Investigation"*, (Doubleday & Company, Inc., Garden City, New York, 1983), p. 77.

[6] Mary T. Clark, *"Augustine of Hippo, Selected Writings"*, (Paulist Press, NY, 1984), p. 269.

(Also. information for John's life taken from *Reader's Digest, "Who's Who in the Bible"*, Pleasantville, NY, 1994.)

Part Two
John 1:1-18

The Incarnation

"In his classic 'A Tale of Two Cities', Charles Dickens summarizes the era of the French Revolution:

'It was the best of times, it was the worst of times, it was the age of wisdom, it was the age of foolishness, it was the epoch of belief, it was the epoch of incredulity, it was the season of light, it was the season of darkness, it was the spring of hope, it was the winter of despair, we had everything before us, we had nothing before us, we were all going direct to Heaven, we were all going direct the other way.'

With this prologue Dickens prefaces his drama. Before the curtain rises, he introduces us to some of the novel's major themes: prosperity and poverty, light and darkness, hope and despair.

John also introduces his Gospel with a prologue. R.C.H. Lenski, in his commentary on the Gospel of John, sees this eighteen-verse introduction as some of the most scintillating writing in the entire New Testament: 'John's is the paragon

9

among the gospels, 'the one, tender, real crown-gospel of them all' (Luther), and the prologue is the central jewel set in pure gold.'

Like Dickens' introduction, John's prologue gives us a glimmer of the book's major themes: the deity of Christ, Christ as light and life, the world shrouded in darkness, the witness of John the Baptist, rejection and acceptance of the Savior, and examples of the glory, grace and truth of Christ."[1]

Cousin John's Prologue

John would have known Jesus personally as a little boy. You see, he was the Lord's cousin. His mother, Salome, was the sister of the Virgin Mary. The strange, and mysterious, and other worldly circumstances surrounding the birth of Jesus in Bethlehem were no secret to the family. Undoubtedly, during his childhood, and early years of manhood, Jesus, along with his brothers, sisters, and cousins would have had normal family contact. Celebrating the feasts and annual pilgrimages to Jerusalem, birthdays along with other special occasions, would have been opportunity to spend time together, laughing, catching up on the latest family news and seeing old friends. When John became a disciple of Jesus, he knew that the virgin-born Jesus of Nazareth was God. In his gospel, he simply tells us what he knows.

In John's prologue, in this statement of thesis there are two parts; first the essential declarations which are found in verses one, fourteen and eighteen; then certain statements which are parenthetical.

> *"In the beginning was the Word, and the Word was with God, and the Word was God." John 1:1*

"And the Word was made flesh, and dwelt among us, and we beheld His glory, the glory as of the only begotten of the Father, full of grace and truth." John 1:14

"No man hath seen God at any time; the only begotten Son, which is in the bosom of the Father, He hath declared Him." John 1:18

Verse One
"In the beginning was the Word"

"Recalls the opening words of *Genesis 1:1: 'In the beginning God created the heavens and the earth.'* The expression does not refer to a particular moment of time but assumes a timeless eternity."[2]

"Word" is the Greek 'logos'. Greek philosophers were familiar with this word. Philo, a Jewish philosopher, borrowed and used this word for his own purposes. The Greek mind used the word as a reference for the abstract components that are foundational to everything that would be considered solid, concrete, a sure foundation. The word "logos", for the Greek would point to what we would call wisdom.

John did not borrow the Greek concept of 'logos", nor did he borrow any of Philo's ideas to describe Jesus. He used a more Hebraic concept. The Hebrews had a more sophisticated approach to the eternal verities behind space and time. The Hebrew would argue from the thought to the thinker, from 'wisdom' to God. The Greeks did not go that far. Thus, when John calls Jesus, 'the Word,' the Logos, he is referring to him as the thinker, the omniscient genius behind the created universe."[3]

"Was", the Greek, is in the imperfect tense, which suggests not something past, present, or future, but something continuous. The idea is an existence that transcends time, that which is

beyond time or space. People measure existence by time. Our point of reference is a point in time, an earmark, a high water mark. The verb John uses takes us beyond this dimension of time, into a timeless sphere of reality. In other words, the One John calls "The Word", "The Logos", doesn't belong to time and space, rather, "The Word" belongs to timelessness, a reality where there is no measure other than God. The "Logos" did not have a beginning, nor will have an ending. The "Word" is eternal. The "Word" is everlasting, without time, space, or measure.

"We can go back in our minds quite easily a century or two, even a millennium or two. Astronomers have accustomed themselves to think in terms of billions of years. But to go back beyond the beginning, to no beginning at all—that is disquieting. But, says John, when we think of Jesus, that is where we must begin. We must go back to the dateless past, to a time before time. We must think of Jesus as never having begun at all. He is eternally God."[4]

"*With*"- Greek 'Pros'—face to face; interfacing; having intercourse; communing; the closest relationship; at home; intimate association with God; partaking of the essence of God; God in triune being; with God; is God. The Greek text stresses description rather than individualization. Meaning this: "the Word was deity, one with God, rather than 'a god' or another being of the same class. This is the real meaning of the phrase. Unity of nature rather than similarity or likeness is implied. The external co-existence and unity of the Word with God is unmistakably asserted."[5]

Verse Fourteen
"And the Word became flesh"

With a few words, John draws the curtain open, and reveals the heart of this new Christian faith, that which is unprecedented in human history, God becoming man to redeem us from our sin, God taking on flesh so that we might understand, believe and receive eternal life.

A New Form

"Became"–"The word refers, not to the beginning of something new, but to that which already had existence, as it became new in manifestation."[6] The "Logos" took on a new form, not a new existence. The birth of the Lord Jesus was unique. When a child is born, it is the creation of a new person, a new personality, someone who has never existed before, a new life. Not so with Jesus. The Word, Logos, or Jesus came into this world, already existing before the world was created, before Mary was born, before the Roman Empire. Jesus was not the creation of a new life, rather the continuance of a person who had existed in eternity past. Jesus did not cease to be God, He simply became human. Completely human, and completely God. This was something profoundly new in the history of the universe that caused Heaven to pause in awe, and the angelic host to sing, blinding earth's sidereal view, rumbling through Judea's hillside with the chorus, "Glory to God in the highest."

There was unity of the God-head before and after the incarnation. Jesus did not cease to be God. At the same time his humanity was real and complete. Jesus remained God as before, but 'He became flesh.'

Jesus - Tabernacle

"Dwelt among us"- Literally meaning "to pitch a tent, to dwell temporarily. Or, He tabernacled among us.

Some believe that because of the word tabernacle, that the incarnation took place on the joyous annual Jewish Feast of Tabernacles. I believe John's use of the word tabernacle points to a rich typology of the Old Testament tabernacle.

Arthur W. Pink states in his work, *"Exposition of the Gospel of John,"*

1. "The tabernacle was a temporary appointment and was used in the wilderness. The wilderness strikingly foreshadowed the conditions amid which the eternal Word tabernacled among men at His first advent. The wilderness home of the tabernacle unmistakably foreshadowed the manger-cradle, the Nazarene's Bench, the "nowhere" for the Son of Man to lay His head, the borrowed tomb for His sepulchre. A careful study of the chronology of the Pentateuch seems to indicate that Israel used the tabernacle in the wilderness…less than 35 years.

2. The tabernacle was God's dwelling place and therefore the place where God met with men. 'There is one Mediator between God and men—the Man Christ Jesus' (1 Timothy 2:5).

3. The tabernacle was the center of Israel's camp. 'Where two or three are gathered together in My name, there am I in the midst of them' (Matthew 18:20).

4. The tabernacle was the place where the Law was preserved. Jesus came to fulfill the Law, not destroy it.

5. The tabernacle was the place where sacrifice was made. The body in which Jesus was tabernacled on earth was nailed to a cross where His precious blood was shed, and where complete atonement was made for sin.

6. The tabernacle was the place where the priestly family was fed and was the place of worship. Jesus is the Bread of Life. He is the One upon whom our soul delights to feed. The Church is God's priestly family today (1 Peter 2:5). Christ is our food, our sustenance.

In terms of worship, it is 'by Him' we are to offer unto God a sacrifice of praise (Hebrews 13:15). It is in Him, and by Him, alone, that we can worship the Father. It is through Him we have access to the throne of grace."[7]

The Tabernacle's glory and beauty was found within. From without, to the eye of the passersby, the structure looked like an ordinary tent set another location apart from the other tents, larger in size, yes, but rather ordinary. The furniture of the outer court was made of brass, or simply copper. The curtains of the outer court were white, bleached by the sun. The only suggestion of beauty was found looking through the gate at the brazen altar. Even when the Tabernacle was moved from place to place the golden furniture that was found within were covered so that no one could behold the splendor of the sacred items.

This reminds us of the hidden glory of Christ Jesus. When he came to "pitch His tent" in the middle of humanity, He did not lay His deity aside, rather He covered His glory among us. The prophet said regarding the Messiah, " He has no form or comeliness; and when we see Him, there is no beauty that we should desire Him" (Isaiah 53:2). The Apostle Paul stated, "Let this mind be in you, which was also in Christ Jesus; Who, being in the form of God, thought it not robbery to be equal with God; But made Himself of no reputation, and took upon Him the form of a servant, and was made in the likeness of men: And being found in fashion as a man, He humbled Himself, and became obedient unto death, even the death of the cross" (Philippians 2:5-8).

"The inside of the tabernacle, seen only by the priests, was glorious. The inner hangings were of blue, purple and scarlet, and were fine linen. All the inner furniture was of gold or overlaid with gold. That mysterious shekinah cloud, which overshadowed the camp of Israel, came to rest on the mercy seat in the Holy of Holies, where it bathed all with the light and glory of another world."[8]

Grace & Truth
"We beheld His glory, the glory as of the only begotten (the one and only) of the Father".

They saw His glory manifested on the Mt. of Transfiguration. This is the same glory that appeared on Mt. Sinai, *"full of grace and truth"*

Moses asked of God, *"...show me thy glory..."* The reply was: *"I will make all my goodness pass before you, and will proclaim before you My name..."* (Exodus 33:18-19)

> *"And the Lord descended in the cloud, and stood with him there, and proclaimed the name of the Lord. And the Lord passed by before him, and proclaimed, the Lord, The Lord God, merciful and gracious, longsuffering, and abundant in goodness and truth" Exodus 34:5,6*

Mercy or Goodness and Truth (Hebrew: Chesed and Emeth) points us to the goodness and the glory of God. The Greek words that John uses in John 1:14 "full of grace (charis), and truth (aletheia)," are understood to be a rendering of the last words of Exodus 34:6. Therefore, the glory seen in Christ, the incarnate Word, was the same glory that was revealed to Moses on Mount Sinai; however, now, that glory became human, fully God & fully man, "full of grace and truth."

"Grace has two basic meanings to it. One, of unmerited and undeserved favor, something we could never achieve, earn or attain. The fact that God came to earth to live and to die for our sins, for atonement. The other reflects the modern Greek meaning of 'charis', meaning charm. Simply, 'in Jesus men are confronted with the sheer loveliness of the love of God.'"[9]

The Hebrew word for truth is *"emet"* which is comprised of the first, middle and last letters of the Hebrew alphabet, aleph, mem & tav, meaning totality. In other words, "truth" embraces the beginning, middle and end of all there is. "Truth" in the gospel of John speaks of the totality of God, or God's reality. Jesus said, "I am the truth," meaning that truth is not simply teaching that comes from Jesus, though it is truth, rather, Jesus Himself is the totality of truth. God, who is the Creator is the only true reality, the reality of God is revealed in the person of Jesus. Therefore, Truth is Christ Jesus, as we are "complete in Him."

The nature of truth is exclusive. The opposite of truth is false. If Jesus is not truth, then He is false. When Pilate asked Jesus, "Art thou the King of the Jews?" Jesus answered him by saying, "Sayest thou this thing of thyself, or did others tell it thee of me? (John 18:33,34) Basically, Jesus was saying to Pilate, "Look deep within your heart Pilate, the answer may be difficult for you to receive. Are you ready to deal with implications of my answer?"

"Pilate therefore said unto him, art thou a king then? Jesus answered, Thou sayest that I am a king. To this end was I born, and for this cause came I into the world, that I should bear witness unto the truth. Every one that is of the truth heareth my voice" (John 18:37).

To reject Jesus is to embrace falsehood, or to believe a lie. Jesus said, "if ye continue in my word, then are ye my disciples indeed; and ye shall know the truth, and the truth shall make you free" (John 8:31-32). The enemy of our soul is the "father of all lies" (John 8:44). He will do anything to keep us from coming to the truth, to God Himself.

Pilate asks, "What is truth?" Notice "no answer is given in words, but the Passion narrative gives the answer in deeds...It is finished! Truth as Jesus understood it was a costly affair."[10]

Verse Eighteen

"No man hath seen God at any time; the only begotten Son, which is in the bosom of the Father, He hath declared Him."

This verse declares what Jesus has revealed. The expression "the bosom of the Father" is a most beautiful and intimate expression, between a child and a parent, or a friend and a friend. The revelation that Jesus came to unveil was nothing less than the heart of God. Jesus could have come as a sage, warrior or king, thus revealing the Father in a different way. Rather, Jesus revealed the bosom of the Father, the heart of God. "For God so loved the world that He gave..." (John 3:16).

"He has declared Him" is from the Greek word, where we derive the term exegesis, which means to explain or interpret. Jesus has made known things that men had not seen.

"The life and words of Jesus are more than an announcement; they are an explanation of God's attitude toward men and of His purpose for them."[11]

Simply, John was saying as we arrange his words...

"In the beginning was the Word and the Word was with God, and the Word was God".

The Birth of God

No one has seen God at any time.

"And the Word became flesh and dwelt (pitched His tent) *among us…full of grace and truth."*

The only begotten Son, who is in the bosom of the Father, He has declared Him.

JESUS IS LORD…JESUS IS TRUTH.

Endnotes

[1] Charles R. Swindoll, *"Exalting Christ, the Son of God, a Study of John 1-5"*, (Insight for Living, 1987), p.9.

[2] Merrill C. Tenney, *"The Expositor's Bible Commentary, John"*, (Zondervan, Grand Rapids, 1981)

[3] John Phillips, *"Exploring the Gospels, John"*, (Loizeauz Brothers, 1989), p. 16

[4] Ibid., p. 17

[5] Merrill C. Tenney, *"The Expositor's Bible Commentary, John"*, (Zondervan, Grand Rapids, 1981), p. 28

[6] G. Campbell Morgan, *"The Gospel According to John"*, (Fleming H. Revell, Westwood, NJ), p. 23

[7] Arthur W. Pink, *"Exposition of the Gospel of John"*, (Zondervan, Grand Rapids, 1975), pp. 34,37

[8] John Phillips, *"Exploring the Gospels, John"*, (Loizeaux Brothers, 1989), p. 27

[9] William Barclay, *"The Gospel of John, Volume One"*, (Westminster Press, Philadelphia, 1956), p. 47

[10] Leon Morris, *"The Gospel According to John"*, (Eerdmans, Grand Rapids, 1995), pp. 260,261

[11] Merrill C. Tenney, *"The Expositor's Bible Commentary, John"*, (Zondervan, Grand Rapids, 1981), p. 34

Part Three
John Chapter One

The Prophet

Author John Phillips writes, "From out of the wilderness had come striding a spiritual giant of a man. His dress, diet, deportment and demands made his hearers think of Elijah. His voice thundered until the windows of conscience rattled in everyone's soul. His eyes flashed like lightning, seeming to read the secrets of everyone's heart.

Multitudes heard about this new prophet and flocked to hear him. The religious establishment investigated him, disliked him, feared him, rejected him and was denounced by him. Herod on his throne was afraid of him. John the Baptist was his name—the son of a priest, (who was) married to the daughter of a priest.

His birth had been foretold. He had been raised strictly, with a view to his becoming a priest. He had also been raised as a Nazarite, with a view to his becoming a prophet. There already were priests after the order of Aaron—enough and to spare. Few and far between were prophets after the order of Elijah. What Israel needed was not another priest.

The Birth of God

What Israel needed was a prophet. John, by birth, training, disposition, conviction and choice was raised up by God to be that prophet, the last of a long, illustrious line."[1]

John's message electrified the nation: 'the Christ is coming! Repent! The kingdom of heaven is at hand!' Thousands throughout the land came to listen to him and were baptized.

John's parents, Zacharias and Elizabeth, were older people, not expecting to have a baby.

> *'And they had no child, because that Elisabeth was barren, and they both were now well stricken in years.'*
> *Luke 1:7*

Luke tells us that John lived in the deserts most of his life.

> *'And the child grew, and waxed strong in spirit, and was in the deserts till the day of his shewing unto Israel.'*
> *Luke 1:80*

John's clothing was that of camel's hair, leather belt and his diet consisted of locusts and wild honey.

> *'And John was clothed with camel's hair, and with a girdle of a skin about his loins; and he did eat locusts and wild honey;' Mark 1:6*

John was the last Old Testament prophet —just a man. There was nothing unique about his name. He was just John…but he was not ordinary. He fulfilled a important purpose.

Sent From God

Verse 6: *"There was a man sent from God, whose name was John."*

"There was a man": The Greek emphasizes, "there appeared on the stage of history, in a specific fixed position in place, time or space."

"Sent from God, whose name was John". John the Baptist was both a priest and Nazarite. "There are only three Nazarites mentioned in the Bible: Samuel, Samson and John the Baptist."

A Nazarite could not touch a dead body, fruit of the vine and had to let his hair grow long. He thus proclaimed to the world that his affections, appetite and appearance were on the altar dedicated to the Lord, thus he kept his body in subjection. This lifestyle was difficult to live. The standard and devotion to God was higher than what the average follower of God could bear. Therefore, in the fifteen hundred years of Jewish history we read only of three who were set apart for God is such a manner. Samson, who failed miserably, was one. The other two, Samuel and John the Baptist, were Hebrew prophets. Samuel was the first of the prophets, and John was the last.

Witnessing the Light

Verse 7:*"The same came for a witness, to bear witness of the Light, that all men through him might believe."*

"Through Him; i.e., through John. It is interesting to note that technically it was John who first pointed men to Jesus as the Light and hope of the World. Subsequently, it was through the belief of these people that others came to believe in Jesus as the

Messiah. Therefore, all believers have, in this sense, been first brought to faith by John.

> Verse 8: *"He was not that Light, but was sent to bear witness of that Light."*

John the Apostle may have been making a strong point to combat those in his day who were making exaggerated claims about John the Baptist.

> Verse 15: *"John bare witness of Him and cried, saying, This was He of whom I spake, He that cometh after me is preferred before me: for He was before me."*

John the Baptist was the first to identify the Lord Jesus for who He really was. He recognized the Lord's pre-existence. The One of old foretold.

The word *"before"* (Greek, protos) "has reference to time—not just to priority of birth, but rather to uniqueness in the matter of time. The Lord Jesus related Himself in time in quite a different way from any other human being. He was related to time as one coming out of eternity. As to His mother, He was born as a baby in Bethlehem; as to His Father, He was 'the Ancient of Days.'"[2]

Who are You?

> Verse 19: *"And this is the record of John, when the Jews sent priests and Levites from Jerusalem to ask him, Who art thou?"*

"Here for the first time we come upon the use of the term 'the Jews' in (John). This term denotes not the people as a whole but one particular group—here, the religious establishment in Jerusalem, whether the Sanhedrin or the temple authorities.

Elsewhere, it is occasionally used (*'After these things Jesus walked in Galilee: for He would not walk in Jewry, because the Jews sought to kill Him.' John 7:1*) to mean the Judeans as distinct from the Galileans, while at other times it has quite a general meaning."[3]

This is the only time we find the two orders, 'priests and Levites', named together in the New Testament. In verse twenty-four we learn that they came from Jerusalem and were sent by the Pharisees.

At this time there was great Messianic expectation and John's ministry was stirring the countryside. John did not fit into any religious mold that was familiar to the Jewish authorities. John's obvious popularity and success demanded an explanation.

> Verse 20-21: *"And he confessed, and denied not; but confessed, I am not the Christ. And they asked him, what then? Art thou Elias? And he saith, I am not. Art thou that prophet? And he answered, no."*

John disclaimed the title of Messiah, meaning anointed. It was a title that associated political freedom from oppressors. Perhaps John did not want to be connected to any political purview. Simply, John did not want to be seen as an insurrectionist. Because of John's roughened exterior many believed him to be Elijah personified. Elijah had challenged Ahab (1 Kings 17-19), and was prophesied to come preparing the way for the Messiah (Malachi 3).

Are you the Prophet? Probably, referring to God's word to Moses:
'The Lord your God will raise up for you a prophet like me from among your own brothers. You must listen to him' (Deuteronomy 18:15). This prophecy said he would be like Moses, therefore the Jews were inquiring whether John would lead them in a New Exodus and overcome the Romans.

It is interesting how John's answers became shorter with each question.

> Verse 22: *"Then said they unto him, Who art thou? That we may give an answer to them that sent us. What sayest thou of thyself?"*

After his denials the delegation from Jerusalem, being greatly frustrated demanded, 'Who are you? What do you say about yourself?'

The Voice

> Verse 23: *"He said, I am the voice of one crying in the wilderness, Make straight the way of the Lord, as said the prophet Esaias."*

"Voice of one…make straight the way…" John was the subject of Old Testament prophecy (*Isaiah 40*). The fortieth chapter of Isaiah deals with prophecies regarding the future. There will be someone who prepares a road for the king through hilly and rugged territory, so that he can travel over a smooth road. John calls himself the "road-builder" for one greater than he, the Messiah. John's birth was miraculous as God intervened (*Luke 1:7, 13*); he was filled with the Holy Spirit from his mother's womb (*Luke 1:15*); he was sent from God (*John 1:6*); he prepared the way of the Lord (*Matthew 3:3*). The Lord said of John, '*… Among them that are born of women there has not risen a greater than John the Baptist…'* (*Matthew 11:11*).

Who are you John? He had quite a resume. However, his purpose was not to draw people to himself, rather, he desired men to follow Jesus, the coming Anointed One.

John was a voice, but he was not the Word. As the Word exists in the mind before the voice articulates, so it was that the Word (Logos) was before the voice.

"Make straight the way of the Lord"

John told us specifically who this One would be. This One who is coming is the Lord. He used the word Jehovah. Jesus of Nazareth, the one born in Bethlehem, is none other than God Himself in flesh, who came to bring redemption, forgiveness and hope.

> Isaiah 40: 1-8: *"Comfort ye, comfort ye my people, saith your God. Speak ye comfortably to Jerusalem, and cry unto her, that her warfare is accomplished, that her iniquity is pardoned: for she hath received of the Lord's hand double for all her sins. The voice of him that crieth in the wilderness, Prepare ye the way of the Lord, make straight in the desert a highway for our God. Every valley shall be exalted, and every mountain and hill shall be made low: and the crooked shall be made straight, and the rough places plain: And the glory of the Lord shall be revealed, and all flesh shall see it together: for the mouth of the Lord hath spoken it. The voice said, Cry. And he said, what shall I cry? All flesh is grass, and all the goodliness thereof is as the flower of the field; The grass withereth, the flower fadeth: because the Spirit of the Lord bloweth upon it: surely the people is grass. The grass withereth, the flower fadeth: but the word of our God shall stand for ever."*

"All flesh is grass" – You may say, "this isn't very comforting." You must understand this is how God begins to comfort us. Because of our pride and selfishness, God must remind us of our lowly estate, our sinfulness, our neediness. God must prick

our conscience to get our attention. That is why Peter bridged Isaiah 40 with the gospel message of redemption.

> *"For all flesh is as grass, and all the glory of man as the flower of grass. The grass withereth, and the flower thereof falleth away: but the word of the Lord endureth for ever. And this is the word which by the gospel is preached unto you." (1 Peter 1: 24,25)*

Why do we need the Lord and to be born again? Because 'that which is born of the flesh is flesh,' and 'all flesh is as grass'. Why do we need a new life? Because we are under judgment, because of sin, and this life is soon going to pass away, and we will stand before God in judgment, as *"it is appointed unto man once to die, but after this the judgment."* Only 'the word of the Lord' endures forever, therefore, we must take heed and recognize how we need life from God, *'He that hath the Son hath life.'*

We can understand how John sees himself in this prophetic passage of Isaiah chapter forty. He says, this is who I am, simply, 'a voice crying in the wilderness.'

> Verse 24, 25: *"And they which were sent were of the Pharisees. And they asked him, and said unto him, why baptizest thou then, if thou be not that Christ, nor Elias, neither that prophet?"*

Isn't that the way it is? What do people do when they are taken out of their comfort zone with a new concept? They raise a ritualistic, familiar technicality.

One Among You

Verse 26: *'John answered them, saying, I baptize with water: but there standeth one among you, whom ye know not;'*

John's reply was succinct, *'I baptize with water. That is all.'*

"The emphatic *'I baptize with water'*, prepares (hearer) for the mention of someone else who will baptize in a different medium. For the moment, John does not speak of this different baptism, but he does speak of the One who will administer it."[4]

The religious leaders knew what John's baptism had meant. An outward sign of their repentance, confession of guilt and their need for remission of sins. But John stated profoundly, *"There stands One among you whom you do not know."* Jesus was standing in the crowd that day, and yet John did not point him out. The reason could have been because Passover was about to begin and John had a special title to bestow upon the Lord. But he did definitely declared, *'there stands One among you…'* (verse 26).

John said he was not the Christ; nor, Elijah; I am not the prophet; however, "I am the voice of one crying in the wilderness," I am preparing the way of the Lord. He did not reveal the mission of the Christ that day. Yes, he affirmed that Christ came. However, he waited until the next day to declare who the Messiah was. *'There stands One among you whom you do not know.'*

Israel was not ready to receive the Message of God's redeeming grace through Jesus Christ our Lord. Also, today, in a post-Christian and post-modern era many are unaware that there is One among (us) whom (they) do not know.

Verse 27: *"He it is, who coming after me is preferred before me, whose shoe's latchet I am not worthy to unloose."*

"John underlines his own relative unimportance in comparison with the Coming One, by saying that he is unfit even to perform such a lowly service as untying His sandal strap for Him. (in Jewish thought), 'Every service which a slave performs for his master, a disciple will perform for his teacher, except to untie his sandal-strap.' Thus, John thought himself unworthy to perform even this act for the Coming One. But, in fact, in preparing the way for the Lord, John was discharging a far more honorable ministry than any of his hearers could have realized."[5]

Beyond Jordan

Verse 28: *"These things were done in Bethabara beyond Jordan, where John was baptizing."*

There is a reason why the Holy Spirit was pleased to tell us where this scene unfolded. Some scholars believe "Bethabara" is the place identical with "Bethbarah", mentioned in Judges 7:24, meaning 'House of Passage', which was so named to memorialize the crossing of the Jordan in the days of Joshua.

'And Gideon sent messengers throughout all Mount Ephraim, saying, Come down against the Midianites, and take before them the waters unto Bethbarah and Jordan. Then all the men of Ephraim gathered themselves together, and took the waters unto Bethbarah and Jordan.' Judges 7:24

It was here, the very same place where the Israelites crossed over the Jordan into the promised land, at a place whose name signified 'House of Passage', a symbol of death, and a symbol of life, that John was baptizing those who confessed and repented from their sins, dying to self, passing out of a false religion into the true faith, thus receiving eternal life. The meaning of this should not be hard to find. Those who believed became part of the remnant who were "prepared for the Lord" (Luke 1:17). So then, the place where John was baptizing was called "The House of Passage".

Behold

> Verses 29-30: *"The next day John seeth Jesus coming unto him, and saith, Behold the Lamb of God, which taketh away the sin of the world. This is He of whom I said, After me cometh a man which is preferred before me: for He was before me."*

About six weeks beforehand, Jesus had been baptized by John in the Jordan river at this very spot. Subsequently the Lord had gone into the Judean wilderness for forty days where He was tempted by Satan. John's picks up the account after the temptation takes place. Jesus has returned to the Jordan and on that day the delegation arrived pressing John for answers. John had seen Jesus in the crowd, however, it wasn't until the next day that John revealed who Jesus was.

At this time of year, Passover was near. This feast commemorated the exodus, Israel's flight from Egypt, the birth of a nation, and redemption by the blood of the lamb. John did not introduce Jesus as the Messiah, Son of Man, nor the Son of God, nor the Word of God. He introduced Jesus as "Lamb of God who takes away the sin of the world." He targeted the heart of everyone's need, redemption. Jesus is the Lamb of God who can redeem you, if you believe.

John's baptism reminded people of their need to repent. However, people need more than just repentance, they need redemption. Water cannot remove the stain of sin, only blood can do that. Not the blood of bulls and goats (Hebrews 10:1-4). Not religion. Only through the precious blood of the Lamb of God can one received redemption.

This title for the Lord, "Lamb", can be found twice in the Old Testament, twice in the gospels, once in the book of Acts, once in the epistles and twenty-eight times in the book of Revelation. Isaac asked the question, as he and his father Abraham headed for the south side of Moriah, "Where is the lamb?" (Genesis 22:7). Abraham answered him, "God will provide Himself a lamb." John answered the question, "Behold the Lamb of God."

As these words came forth from John's mouth you could hear the bleating of Sheep in the background as they were being herded to Jerusalem. These sheep would be used for Passover sacrifice. John is saying in essence. "You hear the sheep in the background? See the sheep? I want you to see and hear the true Passover Lamb. He is the one who can redeem you. Behold, Jesus of Nazareth, the Lamb of God who takes away the sin of the world. It is He who can take away your sins. See Him. Hear Him. Follow Him."

Before Me

> Verse 30: *"This is He of whom I said, After me cometh a man which is preferred before me: for He was before me."*

Notice the word *"Man"* (Greek, *aner*, not *anthropos*).

John repeats verse 15 with exception of the word "Man", which emphasizes not only Christ's mannishness, His humanity, but His headship over His followers. This is the third time John declares that Christ was preferred before him (verses 15, 27, 30). He was affirming Christ's pre-existence.

> Verse 31: *"And I knew him not: but that He should be manifest to Israel, therefore am I come baptizing with water."*

John knew Him, for they were cousins, however he did not know who He was until God revealed it to him.

> Verse 32-33: *"And John bare record, saying, I saw the Spirit descending from heaven like a dove, and it abode upon Him. And I knew Him not: but He that sent me to baptize with water, the same said unto me, Upon whom thou shalt see the Spirit descending, and remaining on Him, the same is He which baptizeth with the Holy Ghost."*

This has reference to the occasion when the Lord himself was baptized by John in the Jordan, when the Father testified to His pleasure, in the Son, and when the Spirit descended upon Him as a dove. The dove manifested the character of the One on whom He came.

The "dove" is a symbol of love and sorrow. This is an appropriate emblem of the Messiah. Both His love and sorrow were manifested at Calvary. Thus, the heavenly Dove bears witness to the mission of Christ. Jesus was the perfect Lamb, and a perfect sacrifice.

In contrast when the Holy Spirit came upon the disciples on the Day of Pentecost, we read there appeared unto them cloven tongues like as of fire, and it sat upon each of them (*Acts 2:3*).

Fire is a symbol divine judgment. There was that in the disciples which needed to be judged. Sin was still present in the disciples, as their evil nature still remained within them. However, there was nothing in the Holy Lamb of God that needed judged. Therefore, the Holy Spirit descended upon Him like a dove, and not as fire.

A New Paradigm

The gospels of Matthew, Mark and Luke mention the Lord Jesus being anointed by the Holy Spirit at His baptism, but John is the only gospel writer that says the Spirit 'abode' or 'remained' upon Him. The Holy Spirit did not come upon Him and then leave again such as in the Old Testament era. The word 'abode' or 'remain' speaks of continuing fellowship, not a temporary moment. The paradigm in universe had shifted, a new era had begun.

John's baptism was an outward sign of inward repentance and confession, but there is a greater baptism.

> *"For John truly baptized with water; but ye shall be baptized with the Holy Ghost not many days hence."*
> *(Acts 1:5)*

This is through trusting in the shed blood of the Lamb of God. Notice again verse 29. Isaiah stated that the Messiah, the Lamb of God, "was wounded for our transgressions, He was bruised for our iniquities: the chastisement of our peace was upon Him; and with His stripes we are healed."

Notice John said "sin" not sins (verse 29). Sins are only the result of a cause – the Fall of Man, and subsequent sin nature. The Lamb of God came not only to take away the individual's sins, but to take away, or deal with the cause of sin as a whole.

The Apostle Paul said, 'God hath made Him to be sin for us, who knew no sin.' He not only bore our sins, and He not only atoned for all our acts of sin, but He died for what we are, sinners.

Whether we like it or not, within the heart of each of us is the propensity to sin. We are capable to flesh out the worse act of sin ever committed. We are sinners by nature. Sin dwells within us. Christ died to put away sin, not merely our sinful acts, through the sacrifice of Himself on the cross. The scripture states we are all sinners. God took that into account as Christ became sin on the cross, who knew no sin. He took our place. He was made sin for us, and sin, this barrier between God and man was taken away. What does this mean? Anyone, even the worst vilest sinner can come into the presence of God and find forgiveness through Christ Jesus. Do you know the Lamb of God who takes away the sin of the world?"

A Declaration of Hope

Verse 34: *"And I saw, and bare record that this is the Son of God."*

John declared seven things:

1. Christ pre-existed in eternity past – verse 15.
2. Christ is Lord – verse 23.
3. Christ is above all – verse 27.
4. Christ is the Passover Lamb – verse 29.
5. Christ is without sin, morally perfect – verse 32.
6. Christ has a divine right to baptize with the Holy Spirit – verse 33.
7. Christ is the Son of God – verse 34.

Oh, how this world needs God's people to stand with a firm conviction as to what they believe, manifesting what it means to be a Christian. Will you take the Banner of Christ as John did and raise it high so that the world will see and believe?

Endnotes

[1] John Phillips, *"Exploring the Gospels, John"*, (Loizeaux Brothers, New Jersey, 1989), p.35.

[2] Ibid., p. 29

[3] F.F. Bruce, *"The Gospel of John"*, (Eerdmans, Grand Rapids, 1983), p. 46

[4] Ibid., pp. 50-51

[5] Ibid., p. 51

Part Four
John Chapter One

A New Movement Begins

Again the next day after John stood, and two of his disciples; And looking upon Jesus as he walked, he saith, Behold the Lamb of God! And the two disciples heard him speak, and they followed Jesus. Then Jesus turned, and saw them following, and saith unto them, What seek ye? They said unto him, Rabbi, (which is to say, being interpreted, Master,) where dwellest thou? He saith unto them, Come and see. They came and saw where he dwelt, and abode with him that day: for it was about the tenth hour. John 1:35-39

Verse 35: *"Next day"*

This is the third day in a series of days. The first day is when the delegation came (1:19). The second day is when John declared Jesus to be the Lamb of God (1:29). This is the third day in which important decisions will be made.

Verse 36: *"Looking at Jesus"* (Greek means "to fix one's gaze" or "to give a penetrating look")

This word occurs only one other time in verse 42, where Jesus beheld Simon and said, "You will be called Cephas." This may have been the last time John the Baptist saw Jesus personally. John's fixed gaze on Jesus was followed by the exclamation, "Behold the Lamb of God." John's disciples will now be directed toward Jesus.

Verse 37: *"Two disciples"*

One was Andrew, the other was John. In the gospel, John speaks as an eyewitness, though he does not directly give his name.

The First Question

Verse 38: *"What do you seek?"*

The Lord, knowing that He was being followed by disciples of John, turned and asked these two awkward fishermen, "What do you seek?" John and Andrew were in awe of the One they were following. John the Baptist, after all, declared Jesus to be the Passover Lamb of God. They had the hutzpah to follow Him but they were probably afraid to speak to Jesus. So Jesus broke the silence with a penetrating question. In essence Jesus was asking, "Why are you seeking me? What do you want?"

"(This) is the very first word that is recorded as falling from the lips of Jesus as He began His public ministry. Here then was and is the first question, the first question of Jesus to a human being. The first question of Jesus to humanity as He begins His ministry. 'What do you seek?' It is a question that plumbs the deepest thing in human life. What are you seeking? What are you seeking? Here in the sanctuary, with the open Bible in front of us, or tomorrow in the store, the office, the home, that is the supreme question. What do we want? What are we seeking?"[1] What are we seeking in life?

Let's Do Lunch

"Where are you staying?" As though Andrew and John were saying "Aah! We don't know. Can we get back with you on that? Where do you live? Perhaps we can come by later and talk about it…let's do lunch." All they knew is that John told them He is the One to follow. So they said, "OK" They were probably in their twenties, not more than thirty years of age.

Verse 39: *"Come and see"*

"Come and see" or "Come, and you will see. The first two words of Jesus in his public ministry were 'What are you seeking?' And, 'Come with Me, and your eyes and heart will be opened, and you will see and understand.'

"Tenth hour" Hebrew time it would be around 4:00 P.M. or Roman time it was 10:00 A.M.. This moment was so significant for John that he records the actual time that he surrendered to Christ. Do you remember when you were first encountered the Savior? Do you remember the moment you believed?

Got to Tell Somebody

"One of the two which heard John speak, and followed him, was Andrew, Simon Peter's brother. He first findeth his own brother Simon, and saith unto him, We have found the Messias, which is, being interpreted, the Christ. And he brought him to Jesus. John 1:40-42a

"We look first at how Peter was drawn to Jesus. One can picture Andrew and John hurrying away from this momentous meeting. Andrew is saying, 'I must tell Simon'. John is saying, 'I'm going to get James. I've got to tell somebody'. 'He first found his own brother' can legitimately be rephrased, 'Andrew found first his own brother.' The implication is that Andrew found his brother first, that is, before John found his brother.

It is well within the meaning of the text that both Andrew and John brought a brother to Jesus but that Andrew was first to do so. 'And he brought him to Jesus', John says. This is characteristic of John telling us about Andrew's convert rather than his own. Andrew's convert became the first messenger of the church, Peter (Acts2); John's convert, James, became the first martyr among the apostles."[2]

Never the Same

"And when Jesus beheld him, He said, Thou art Simon the son of Jona: thou shalt be called Cephas, which is by interpretation, A stone." John 1:42b

"You will be called Cephas" was a discription of Peter's personality. Simon, or Simeon, was the name of Jacob's second oldest son (Genesis 29:33), who, with his brother Levi, had brutally avenged the defilement of their sister by a Canaanite prince. The brutish and impulsive propensity of Simeon was echoed in Simon. This characteristic is recorded for us in all the gospels, as we can clearly see his reckless temper manifested (John 18:10).

The name Cephas is an Aramaic name. Peter is the Greek name. Both means rock, or stone. Jesus was saying "Simon, you can become Cephas or Peter if you follow me." The gospels and history confirms the growth and development of the apostle. Peter was someone you could not depend on. He was unpredictble. Nevertheless, the Lord's eyes gazed deeply, piercing the eyes of Simon's. Simon could not escape, the Lord captured him. Although Simon Peter almost fell away, he never did. The principle is clear. When we follow Jesus, we change for the better. We are never the same.

> Verses 43,44: *"The day following Jesus would go forth into Galilee, and findeth Philip, and saith unto him, Follow me. Now Philip was of Bethsaida, the city of Andrew and Peter."*

The Fourth Day

"The following day"

Day 1 – Delegation came; Day 2 – John's declaration; Day 3 – Andrew, John, Peter – Now it is day four.

"He found Philip"

Notice the different methods of evangelism used:

1. The approach used for Andrew and John was "mass evangelism". The message was Jesus is the Lamb of God. They heard the message, they followed Christ.

2. Peter's conversion was a result of "personal evangelism" when Andrew found him and stated, "We have found the Messiah", and brought Peter to Jesus.

3. Philip's conversion was a result of "cold-contact evangelism". Jesus confronted Philip on the street. No

one really attempted to witness to Philip. Jesus found him. This is a profound truth. Jesus finds us.

"We love Him, because He first loved us." 1 John 4:19.

"Follow Me"

This is the first time, as far as the record tells us, that Jesus uttered this formula He so loved to use. "Follow Me" or "Come and travel with Me", "Come and journey with Me". Perhaps Jesus put His arm around Philip or on his shoulder with sincerity in His voice and probably with a smile…said "Come with Me".

We are on an adventure with Jesus. On a journey that embraces challenge, trial, rejection from the world, tribulation, sacrifice, denial. But also you will find meaning, purpose of life and ultimately fulfillment and peace and above all eternal life with God through Christ.

"Bethsaida" means "house of fishing". Home also to Andrew and Peter. It was near the Sea of Galilee.

See For Yourself

Verse 45: *"Philip findeth Nathanael, and saith unto him, We have found him, of whom Moses in the law, and the prophets, did write, Jesus of Nazareth, the son of Joseph."*

Philip with great enthusiasm found his friend Nathanael. His method of evangelism resembled Andrew's, perhaps with more emphasis using Scripture.

Nathanael was a student of the Hebrew Scriptures. He knew the Messiah would be born in Bethlehem. He poured over the prophecies. He knew the requirements. He was astonished at his friends enthusiasm about Jesus of Nazareth, the son of Joseph. Notice his response…

> Verse 46: *"And Nathanael said unto him, Can there any good thing come out of Nazareth? Philip saith unto him, Come and see."*

Nathanael came from Cana of Galilee (John 21:2), less than five miles from Nazareth. There was great prejudice against the little town of Nazareth. It was a backwoods town with a mixture of Gentile and Jewish residents. It had a poor reputation of being unsophisticated.

Because of "the coarseness of its dialect, the people from Judea held Galilee in low esteem. Jesus had an accent. Nathanael perhaps hedging for a time. Jesus, the Messiah? The son of Joseph? Surely not. From Nazareth? Impossible!

Nazareth, in the gospels, lived up to its reputation. It was the first city to greet Jesus' claims with violence, and was ready to put Him to death on the strength of just one day's exposure to His teaching. He was actively hindered in ministry there because of the town's scornful rejection of His claims."[3]

Philip said, "Come and see for yourself…"

Finding God

> Verses 47, 48: *"Jesus saw Nathanael coming to him, and saith of him, Behold an Israelite indeed, in whom is no guile! Nathanael saith unto him, Whence knowest thou me? Jesus answered and said unto him, Before that Philip called thee, when thou wast under the fig tree, I saw thee."*

The Lord saw into Nathanael's soul. Speaking not to Nathanael but to the others he said, 'Behold an Israelite indeed, in whom is no guile' (or deceit). Guile can be translated Jacob. He is not like Jacob. Jacob was a man of deceit in his early years, until God broke him physically and spiritually at Jabbok and changed him into Israel.

"After fleeing his uncle Laban's house, Jacob learns that his brother Esau is marching toward him (with 400 troops). Jacob is very frightened. Jacob cannot forget that when they last saw each other, Esau was plotting to murder him in revenge for Jacob's having deceptively procured from Isaac the blessing intended for Esau. That night while sleeping, Jacob is attacked by a man…and wrestled with him all night…Although (this man) is other-worldly (and) wounds him in the thigh, Jacob ultimately succeeds in pinning the man, refusing to free him until he gives him a blessing. The man awards Jacob with the additional name of Israel (Yisra'el) meaning 'you have wrestled with God and with men and prevailed'. The Jewish people, descendants from Jacob's twelve sons…eventually become known as B'nai Yisra'el, the children of Israel."[4]

Nathanael said, "How do you know me?" He agreed with the Lord's evaluation of his character. Nathanael was astounded as to how the Lord knew him.

"Before"

Simply before I knew you…before the foundation of the world I knew you.

"Under the fig tree I saw you"…

This phrase is found in rabbinic literature and is used in the context of meditation on the Law. Students of Scripture would try to find a quiet place to study and meditate. The Lord's words imply that Jesus knew what Nathanael was thinking about, what he was meditating on. He was thinking about Jacob and the Genesis story of Jacob's ladder, the night Jacob was converted.

> *"And Jacob went out from Beersheba, and went toward Haran. And he lighted upon a certain place, and tarried there all night, because the sun was set; and he took of the stones of that place, and put them for his pillows, and lay down in that place to sleep. And he dreamed, and behold a ladder set up on the earth, and the top of it reached to heaven: and behold the angels of God ascending and descending on it. And, behold, the Lord stood above it, and said, I am the Lord God of Abraham thy father, and the God of Isaac: the land whereon thou liest, to thee will I give it, and to thy seed; And thy seed shall be as the dust of the earth, and thou shalt spread abroad to the west, and to the east, and to the north, and to the south: and in thee and in thy seed shall all the families of the earth be blessed. And, behold, I am with thee, and will keep thee in all places whither thou goest, and will bring thee again into this land; for I will not leave thee, until I have done that which I have spoken to thee of. And Jacob awaked out of his sleep, and he said, Surely the Lord is in this place; and I knew it not. And he was afraid, and said, How dreadful is this place! this is none other but the house of God, and this is the gate of heaven. And Jacob rose up early in the morning, and took the stone that he had put for his pillows, and set it up for a pillar, and poured oil upon the top of it. And he called the name of that place Bethel: but the name of that city was called Luz at the first. And Jacob vowed a vow, saying, If God will be with me, and will keep me in this way that I go, and will give me bread to eat, and raiment to put on, So that I come again to my father's house in peace; then shall the Lord be my God: And this*

44

stone, which I have set for a pillar, shall be God's house:
and of all that thou shalt give me I will surely give the
tenth unto thee." Genesis 28:10-22

David very wisely counseled his son, Solomon, concerning God:

"If you seek Him, He will let you find Him..." 1
Chronicles 28:9

This is what Nathanael was doing. This was true for Nathanael and it can be true for you. You seek Christ and you will find Him.

"Jacob was filled with guile (deceit) and had been forced to leave home because he had lied to his father and swindled his brother. If under these circumstances Jacob was eligible for a revelation from God, would not Nathanael be even more worthy of such a blessing? Jesus said that Nathanael was free from deceit and used the imagery of Jacob's dream to describe the greater revelation He would give to Nathanael... Jesus implied that He Himself would be the medium of that revelation, and His order of the angel's procedure implies that they rose from earth to heaven with their inquiries and then returned to earth with the answers. The Lord's mission is to answer human need and to make sure that the answers are proclaimed."[5]

The fig tree is also usually a symbol of Israel as a nation in a fruitless state of unbelief under the old covenant. Nathanael represents part of the godly remnant in the nation who will come into the blessing of the new covenant by faith in Messiah Jesus.

Amen, Amen!

Verses 49-51: *"Nathanael answered and saith unto him, Rabbi, thou art the Son of God; thou art the King of Israel. Jesus answered and said unto him, Because I said unto thee, I saw thee under the fig tree, believest thou? Thou shalt see greater things than these. And he saith unto him, Verily, verily, I say unto you, Hereafter ye shall see heaven open, and the angels of God ascending and descending upon the Son of man."*

Verse 51 *"Most assuredly" "Verily, verily", said Jesus. Truly, truly or Amen, Amen (Hebrew Amane).*

The word "'Amen' is a Hebrew word with roots in the ordinary Hebrew for belief, faithfulness and truth. It is found closing the first book of Psalms: 'Amen and Amen' (Psalms 41:13)... The double 'Amen' is used for solemn emphasis, to express the assurance that the prayer embodied in this doxology psalm would be answered. The same 'Amen, and Amen' closes the second book of Psalms 72:19 and also the third book (Psalms 89:52). The fourth book ends with a single 'Amen' and then, 'Praise ye the Lord' (Psalms 106:48). The final book of Psalms ends with five psalms each beginning and ending with another great Hebrew word, 'Hallelujah', 'Praise ye the Lord'.

It is interesting that John records the word 'Amen' in the apocalypse as a name of Christ (Revelation 1:18; 3:14). It is the name by which He addressed Himself to the lukewarm, end-time, Laodicean church. The word 'Amen' is also the last word in the Bible. The last thing God has to say to us is to leave us pondering a word that is a name for his beloved Son:

"The grace of our Lord Jesus Christ be with you all. Amen." Revelation 22:21

Thus grace and truth did indeed come by Jesus Christ and, after affirming that, God has no more to say. The double 'Amen', is used to emphasize the Lord's divine authority to mark the importance of what He was about to say, and to affirm the certainty of the truth He declared."[6]

Ladders and Angels

The double "amen" got Nathanael's attention. It reminded him of Jacob's conversion and the ladder with the angels ascending and descending from heaven to earth. Jesus was saying, Nathanael, "I am the ladder that links heaven and earth, God and man. I am the way to heaven. You have called me the Son of God. I am! You have called me the King of Israel. I am! I am the only way to God. The angels ascend and descend in celebration of me."

Notice the angels are ascending and descending. Not descending and ascending. They are already here. They are stationed in every corner, every state, every country, every where people are located. Satan can't do anything about them. They are here for various reasons and they are in constant communication with heaven's command.

There are guardian angels who watch over children. Jesus said, "Take heed that ye despise not one of these little ones; for I say unto you, that in heaven their angels do always behold the face of My Father which is in heaven. (Matthew 18:10) These angels ascend this glorious stairway, heavily burdened, reporting before a Holy God, cases of child abuse, neglected, rejected and aborted. Then they descend with their new orders from their commander and chief to care for the little ones assigned to them, to watch over and to protect and defend.

There are angels who are assigned to God's own people, over churches. Some reports are not good. But, thankfully, there are good reports of faithfulness and revival. Do you ever wonder what they report about you?

Who is Jesus?

"Son of man" has varying levels of emphasis. One of which is a title for the millennial kingdom in which the Son of man will sit on the throne in Jerusalem as King of Israel. There will be open communication between the Heavenly Jerusalem and the earthly. Jesus is the glory of both.

"The title 'Son of man' appears twelve times in the Gospel of John…As the 'Son of man' Jesus reveals divine truth (John 1:51); He has a supernatural origin (John 3:13; 6:62); His death by being 'lifted up' achieves salvation for men (John 3:14; 8:28; 12:34); He exercises the prerogative of final judgement (John 5:27); and He provides spiritual nourishment (John 6:27).

This title is also used of His being glorified (John 12:23; 13:31), which John applies specifically to death and resurrection (John 7:39; 12:16)…

In its general usage it is the title of the incarnate Christ who is the representative of humanity before God and the representative of deity in human life. In the perfection of Christ's humanity, God finds the fullness of His expression to men."[7]

> *"And he is before all things, and by him all things consist."* Colossians 1:17

> *"For it pleased the Father that in him should all fullness dwell;"* Colossians 1:19

"For in him dwelleth all the fullness of the Godhead bodily. And ye are complete in him, which is the head of all principality and power:" Colossians 2:9,10

"...Christ is all, and in all." Colossians 3:11b

The Son of man, being Jacob's ladder, is God's link with earth.

"I saw in the night visions, and, behold, one like the Son of man came with the clouds of heaven, and came to the Ancient of days, and they brought him near before him." Daniel 7:13

"Jesus saith unto him, Thou hast said: nevertheless I say unto you, Hereafter shall ye see the Son of man sitting on the right hand of power, and coming in the clouds of heaven." Matthew 26:64

Are you connected with Him? Do you believe? Are you traveling with Him? Are you His disciple? Or are you still waffling in decision? Make a decision today.

Without Christ, you have no hope. He is our link to God and to eternal life.

What do you seek? What are you seeking? What are you seeking in life?

Jesus said, "Follow Me". Come and travel with Me. Come and journey with Me. He is the Son of man. He is all and in all. He is all you need. You can be complete in Him! He is our fortress and strength. He is life itself.

Dr. Jeffrey D. Johnson

Endnotes

[1] G. Campbell Morgan, *"The Gospel According to John"*, (Fleming Revell), p. 43.

[2] Phillips, *"Exploring the Gospels, John"*, *(Loizeaux Brothers, 1989)* pp. 44,45.

[3] Ibid., p. 47.

[4] Telushkin, *"Jewish Literacy"*, (Morrow, 1981), pp. 39,40.

[5] Gaebelein, *"The Expositor's Bible Commentary, John, Acts"*, (Zondervan, 1981), p. 41.

[6] Phillips, *"Exploring the Gospels, John"*, (Loizeaux Brothers, 1989), pp. 48,49.

[7] Gaebelein,, *"The Expositor's Bible Commentary, John, Acts"*, (Zondervan, 1981), p. 141.

www.ingramcontent.com/pod-product-compliance
Lightning Source LLC
Chambersburg PA
CBHW070831100426
42813CB00003B/567